WOOLLY RHINOCEROS

BY ELIZABETH NEUENFELDT
ILLUSTRATIONS BY MAT EDWARDS

EPIC

EPIC, AN IMPRINT OF BELLWETHER MEDIA BY FLUTTERBEE

EPIC BOOKS are no ordinary books. They burst with intense action, high-speed heroics, and shadows of the unknown. Are you ready for an Epic adventure?

This edition first published in 2026 by Bellwether Media, Inc.

For information regarding permission, write to Bellwether Media, Inc., Attention: Permissions Department, 3500 American Blvd W, Suite 150, Bloomington, MN 55431.

Library of Congress Cataloging-in-Publication Data is available at www.loc.gov or upon request from the publisher.

ISBN: 9798893048193 (hardcover)
ISBN: 9798893049190 (ebook)

Editor: Betsy Rathburn Designer: Jeffrey Kollock

Printed in the United States of America, North Mankato, MN.

TABLE OF CONTENTS

WHAT WAS THE WOOLLY RHINOCEROS?

The woolly rhinoceros was a kind of rhino. These **mammals** had woolly fur and big horns.

They first appeared around three million years ago. This was during the **Pliocene epoch**.

Woolly rhinos were around 6 feet (2 meters) tall at the shoulders. They were about 12 feet (4 meters) long.

Most had two horns on their heads. The front horn was very long. The back horn was shorter.

Woolly rhinos lived in northern **grasslands**. It was very cold. Thick fur kept them warm. Their small ears kept in heat.

A hump on their backs stored fat. It helped them live when food was low.

hump

THE LIFE OF THE WOOLLY RHINOCEROS

Woolly rhinos were **herbivores**. Their diet likely changed with the seasons. They ate **forbs** and grasses in summer.

WOOLLY RHINOCEROS DIET

They ate woody plants in winter. They used their horns to uncover plants under snow.

Woolly rhinos likely lived alone. They may have been **territorial**. They likely fought one another.

They may have lived in small groups to raise **calves**. In warmer times, groups moved farther north.

Woolly rhinos were hunted by early humans. Young rhinos were also hunted by cave lions and cave hyenas.

RHINO RESOURCES

Humans hunted woolly rhinos for their meat, fur, and horns. They made sharp tools from the horns.

Woolly rhinos fought back with their horns.

FOSSILS AND EXTINCTION

Woolly rhinos went **extinct** up to 14,000 years ago. They likely died out from changes in the **climate**. Humans may have also overhunted them.

People have found many woolly rhino **fossils**. They have even found **preserved** remains!

PRESERVED WOOLLY RHINOCEROS CALF

NICKNAME
Sasha

DATE FOUND
around 2015

WHERE
Abyysky District, Siberia, Russia

FOSSIL FINDS
Around 1,200 woolly rhino fossils have been found so far!

Studies show woolly rhinos are related to Sumatran rhinos.
WOOLLY RHINOCEROS
reddish-brown fur
two larger horns
larger body
more fur

Both animals have two horns and fur. But Sumatran rhinos have less fur. They have **adapted** well to their warm homes!

SUMATRAN RHINOCEROS

GET TO KNOW THE WOOLLY RHINOCEROS

WHEN DID THEY LIVE?
around 3 million years ago
Woolly rhinoceroses first appear
160,000 to 90,000 years ago
Early modern humans first appear
up to 14,000 years ago
Woolly rhinoceroses go extinct
two horns
small ears
HEIGHT
around 6 feet (2 meters) at the shoulder
WHERE DID THEY LIVE?
Europe and Asia

GLOSSARY

adapted—changed over a long period of time

calves—baby woolly rhinoceroses

climate—the long-term weather in a particular place

extinct—no longer living

forbs—herbs other than grass; herbs are the leaves of some types of plants.

fossils—the remains of things that lived long ago

grasslands—lands covered with grasses and other soft plants with few bushes or trees

herbivores—animals that only eat plants

mammals—warm-blooded animals that have backbones and feed their young milk

Pliocene epoch—a time in history that lasted from 5.3 million to 2.6 million years ago

preserved—kept safe from being damaged or destroyed

territorial—wanting to keep an area safe

TO LEARN MORE

AT THE LIBRARY

Kington, Emily. *Rhinos*. Truro, U.K.: Hungry Tomato, 2022.

Murray, Julie. *Rhinoceros*. Minneapolis, Minn.: Abdo Zoom, 2022.

Neuenfeldt, Elizabeth. *Woolly Mammoths*. Minneapolis, Minn.: Bellwether Media, 2025.

ON THE WEB

FACTSURFER

Factsurfer.com gives you a safe, fun way to find more information.

1. Go to www.factsurfer.com.

2. Enter "woolly rhinoceros" into the search box and click 🔍.

3. Select your book cover to see a list of related content.

INDEX

The images in this book are reproduced through the courtesy of: Mat Edwards, front cover, pp. 1, 4-5, 6-7, 8-9, 10-11, 12-13, 14-15, 16-17, 18-19, 20-21.